The Open University
A second level course
Popular culture Block 1 Unit 3

Popular culture: themes and issues (2)

Unit 3 Popular culture: history and theory
Tony Bennett

The Open University Press

The Open University Press
Walton Hall, Milton Keynes
MK7 6AA

First published 1981

Designed by the Graphic Design Group of the Open University.

Set in 10/12 pt Sabon at Filmtype Services Limited, Scarborough.

Printed in England by Pindar Print Limited, Scarborough, North Yorkshire.

ISBN 0 335 10121 6

This text forms part of an Open University course. The complete list of units in the course appears at the end of this text.

For general availability of supporting material referred to in this text, please write to: Open University Educational Enterprises Limited, 12 Cofferidge Close, Stony Stratford, Milton Keynes MK11 1BY, Great Britain.

Further information on Open University courses may be obtained from the Admissions Office, The Open University, P.O. Box 48, Walton Hall, Milton Keynes MK7 6AB.

1.1

Unit 3   Popular culture: history and theory

Contents

Set reading

Extracts from Hoggart, R. *The Uses of Literacy*, which are reprinted in Offprints Booklet 1.
The following readings are all in Bennett, T., Martin, G., Mercer, C. and Woollacott, J. (eds) (1981) *Culture, Ideology and Social Process*, Batsford (Reader 2):
Williams, R. 'The analysis of culture'
Volosinov, V.N. 'The study of ideologies and philosophy of language'
Introduction to the 'Passages from Gramsci'
Gramsci, A. 'Hegemony'

Recommended reading

Chapter 1 of Hebdige, D. *Subculture: The Meaning of Style* (set book).

Popular culture: history and theory

1 Introduction

My principal concern in this unit is to outline some of the more important theoretical controversies which currently characterize the study of popular culture in this country and, however approximately, to place these in some kind of historical perspective. An obvious difficulty here consists in the interdisciplinary nature of popular culture as a field of study. Its subject matter clearly involves all the traditional arts-based disciplines – history, music, literature, art history – to which, in recent years, there have been added the new areas of inquiry developed in relation to the mass media: film and television studies, for example. Further, the extended usage of the concept of culture as referring to 'the whole way of life' of a particular social group or class clearly opens up the area to the contributions of such disciplines as sociology and anthropology. Clearly it will not be possible here to trace the development of the study of popular culture within each of these disciplines. Fortunately this is not necessary since the concerns that have been addressed within the different disciplines have been derived largely from wider, interdisciplinary bodies of theory, with the result that there has usually been a good deal of common ground between them.

So far as these wider governing analytical frameworks or *paradigms* are concerned, the study of popular culture in Britain has gone through two critical stages. The first, difficult to pin down precisely, took form during the mid to late nineteenth century. This moment in the history of the study of popular culture was absolutely epochal. It departed significantly from earlier discussions of popular recreations and, albeit with some modifications, specified the terms of debate that were to dominate the discussion for more than a century. The most important founding figure of this moment in the 'history of the theory' was undoubtedly Matthew Arnold whose *Culture and Anarchy*, first published in 1869, articulated concerns that were to remain at the forefront of debate until the 1950s. However, special mention must also be made of the new lease of life that was injected into the Arnoldian heritage in the 1930s by T.S Eliot and, perhaps with greater influence, by F.R. Leavis and the like-minded intellectuals – Q.D. Leavis, L.C. Knights and Denys Thompson, for example – associated with *Scrutiny*, a journal of literary criticism edited by Leavis. Within this tradition, which I shall call the 'culture and civilization' tradition, the new forms of popular culture associated with the development of industrial capitalism – the popular press, the penny-dreadful and the cinema – were grouped under the category of 'mass culture' and, for the greater part, were viewed with disquiet so far as their consequences for the general standards of culture and civilization were concerned. The tradition, was in this sense, culturally conservative, the newer forms of popular culture being contrasted unfavourably with both earlier forms of popular culture and with the exacting standards which the critics concerned required of high culture. However, political concerns were also involved in these cultural concerns inasmuch as it was feared that the dilution and the debasement of the cultural diet of the people attributable to the development of 'mass culture' coinciding, as it did, with the extension of the political franchise, augered ill for the continued maintenance of social and political order. Put simply, it was feared that the people, having been granted – or having won – a formal political role, were being ill-equipped, culturally, to perform that role responsibly.

There were, of course, developments in particular disciplines which, if they did not exactly challenge the dominance of the 'culture and civilization' tradition, at least in part escaped or stood to one side of its gravitational pull. But these were few and far between and their impact was marginal. Even as late as the mid-fifties, the 'culture and civilization' tradition provided, in the form of 'Leavisism', the only developed intellectual terrain on which it was possible to engage with the study of popular culture. Historically, of course, the work produced by the 'Leavisites' was of seminal importance, constituting the first attempt to apply to popular forms techniques of literary analysis previously reserved for 'serious' works. In 1933, Leavis and Thompson significantly extended the range of interest of concerned criticism by studying advertisements in this way in *Culture and Environment* (see Unit 14). Q.D. Leavis provided a similar service for popular fiction in *Fiction and the Reading Public*, first published in 1932. Perhaps more importantly, the general impact of 'Leavisism' – at least as scathing in its criticisms of established 'high' and 'middle-brow' culture as of popular forms – tended to unsettle the prevailing canons of aesthetic judgement and evaluation with, in the long term, quite radical and often unforeseen consequences.

Nonetheless, there is also a sense in which the stance adopted in relation to popular culture actively impeded its development as an area of study. For the operative terms of the 'culture and civilization' tradition, contrasting 'mass culture' unfavourably with earlier forms of 'folk culture', constituted an already worked-out theory of cultural decline which further research could merely confirm, qualify, extend or develop, but not – at least not without breaking with the theory – challenge effectively. It was an assumption of the theory that there was something wrong with popular culture and, of course, once that assumption had been made, all the rest followed: one found what one was looking for – signs of decay and deterioration – precisely because the theory required that these be found. In short, the only role offered to the products of popular culture was that of fall-guy. They existed only in order to be condemned, to be found wanting on one ground or another: as corrosive of the capacity for ethical and aesthetic discrimination, or – and most enduringly – as worse than whatever forms of popular culture may have preceded them, a corruption and dilution of an earlier and supposedly sturdier, more robust and organic phase in the development of the people's culture.

Perhaps what most needs to be stressed, however, is that throughout the 'culture and civilization' tradition only a very few attempts were made to examine – in a detailed and rigorous way which would take account of their real complexity as well as of the manifold differences between them – the actual products of popular culture. In part this was a product of cultural reflexes. The 'culture and civilization' tradition was very much a discourse of the 'cultured' about the culture of those without 'culture'. And it showed. The business of leaving the vaunting heights of high culture to visit the cultural wastelands beneath them was clearly viewed as a wearisome, regrettable necessity. It had to be done, the visit had to be made if but to confirm – yet again – that the heights and the wastelands were, indeed, different. In short, popular culture was approached from a distance and gingerly, held out at arm's length by outsiders who clearly lacked any sense of fondness for or participation in the forms they were studying. It was always the culture of 'other people' that was at issue.

The situation has changed virtually beyond recognition over the last twenty-five years. The intellectual climate prevailing in institutions of higher education in the fifties was such that degree or even sub-degree courses in the area of popular culture would have been unthinkable. 'Culture' was, unquestionably and unequivocally, the monopoly of university arts and humanities departments and, if one wanted to study or acquire it, that was where one went. The study of popular culture now, by contrast, enjoys a well established place in most institutions of higher education. More importantly perhaps, the ways and contexts in which it is studied have also changed. The sense of 'cultural slumming' that characterized earlier contributions, for example, has virtually disappeared. The significant expansion of higher education and the corresponding change in the social composition of the student and teaching bodies, combined with the more generalized social presence exerted by popular culture in Britain since the Second World War, have meant that to study popular culture is no longer to study the culture of 'other people'. This has altered the entire tone of the debate as a sense of liking for and, often, deep involvement in the forms studied has replaced the aloof and distant approach 'from above', and as the need to *understand* the effects of popular culture on ourselves has displaced the need to *condemn* it because of what it does to 'other people'.

More important, perhaps, this increased interest in the study of popular culture has been accompanied by a significant shift in the terms of theoretical reference governing the way in which it is conducted. It is customary to refer to these new lines of approach as the 'cultural studies' approach. This is defined, in part, by the fact that the approach brings together the contributions of diverse disciplines – history, politics, sociology, television and film studies, art history, literary criticism – in a joint concern with the interaction between culture and politics in a way that has seriously challenged the conventional boundary lines between disciplines. However, what most marks the transition between the two approaches is the fact that, in contrast with the conservative concerns expressed within the 'culture and civilization' tradition, the way in which culture and politics have been connected within the 'cultural studies' approach has, for the greater part, been influenced by developments within Marxist theory. It must be added, however, that the Marxism which informs the cultural studies approach is a *critical* Marxism in the sense that it has contested the reductionist implications of earlier Marxist approaches to the study of culture. These, especially in Britain, often tended to view culture – whether we mean this in the sense of works of art or literature, or the ways of life of particular social classes – as being totally determined by economic relationships. The Marxist approaches that have informed the development of the cultural studies perspective, by contrast, have insisted on the 'relative autonomy' of culture – on the fact that it is not simply dependent on economic relationships and cannot, accordingly, be reduced to or viewed as a mere reflection of these, and that it actively influences and has consequences for economic and political relationships rather than simply being passively influenced by them.

The situation is complicated, however, by the fact that there are, in the main, two different routes through which such critical perspectives have been developed. The first, very much a home-grown tradition, has emerged from the work of historians such as Edward Thompson, whose *The Making of the English Working Class* seriously undermined the view that the culture of the nineteenth-century working class could be viewed as a mere reflex of its economic position, and from the works of Raymond Williams who, since the publication of *Culture and Society* in 1958, has consistently argued against such reductionist approaches to the study of culture and for that more extended concept of culture as the study, not merely of works of art, but of the 'relationships between elements in a whole way of life' (Williams, 1965, p.47 in Reader 2). Since the mid-sixties, this indigenous tradition of Marxist theory has been complemented by a variety of European-based Marxist traditions. The more important of these, from the point of view of our concerns here, are those currents of French thought influenced by the development of semiology, which might be defined, in shorthand, as a 'science of the life of signs in society'. The most distinguishing characteristic of such approaches is their application of techniques and methods derived from linguistics to the study of cultural forms as diverse as wrestling matches, styles of dress and the rules governing eating or drinking customs on the one hand, and the novels of Balzac or the theatre of Pirandello on the other.

Opinions have varied as to how the relationships between these two traditions – known, by convention, as the 'culturalist' and the 'structuralist' approaches – should be viewed. Although some have argued that there are implacable differences between them, others have argued that the two both have informed and influenced one another, and that they should continue to do so. Whichever position is adopted, however, it is usually agreed that there are important differences between the two approaches, and ones that cannot easily be reconciled. This situation has been complicated further in recent years by the influence of the work of Antonio Gramsci, an Italian Marxist whose concept of hegemony suggests lines of approach to the study of popular culture which differ significantly from those contained in both the 'culturalist' and the 'structuralist' perspectives.

The above then, in broad canvas, constitute the main shifts that have taken place in the development of the study of popular culture in Britain. In the rest of this unit I shall deal with each of these in greater detail. My aims in doing so are:

1   to identify more fully the political concerns that were expressed and worked through within the 'culture and civilization' tradition;
2   to relate these to developments within the sphere of popular culture itself;
3   to account for the transition from the 'culture and civilization' to the 'cultural studies' approach to the study of popular culture;
4   to outline the points at issue between the 'culturalist' and the 'structuralist' approaches;
5   to introduce Gramsci's concept of hegemony and outline its relevance to the study of popular culture.

In the course of dealing with these aims, I shall also be seeking to further your understanding of the problems of definition introduced in Units 1/2 *Popular culture: defining our terms*. I shall, in particular, be concerned with the light that the historical development of popular culture may throw upon the problem of the historical range and application of the term. My contention here will be that it is indeed helpful to stress the differences rather than the continuities between pre- and post-industrial forms of popular culture. I shall also outline the position, introduced at the end of

Units 1/2, according to which popular culture is viewed as an *area of exchange* between classes, because this is the sense in which, for the most part, the term will be used in this course.

2 The abuses of literacy

I want you now to get some 'feel' of the issues that are identified in abstract terms in the preceding section by reading two sections from Hoggart's *The Uses of Literacy*. This has customarily been regarded as a dividing of the ways in the post-war study of popular culture, pointing back to the concerns of the 'culture and civilization' approach as well as forward to the cultural studies approach. I want you to work out how.

The book is divided into two parts. The first consists of Hoggart's account of the working-class culture of his childhood. This is presented as a culture which, having its origins in the first industrializing and urbanizing experience of the 1830s, had achieved its fully stable and finally perfected form – as the product of three generations of urban and industrial life and of one generation of literacy on an extended basis throughout the class – by the 1930s, the period of Hoggart's childhood. By the 1950s, this culture is viewed as being threatened by newer forms of mass entertainment.

You should now read the two extracts from *The Uses of Literacy* contained in Offprint Booklet 1. The first relates to the working-class culture of the 1930s; the second is concerned with the 1950s. In reading these, try to answer the following questions.

1   What differences are there between the ways in which the relationships between commercially produced forms of popular entertainment and the culture as a 'whole way of life' of the working class are viewed in the two periods?

2   How are the relationships between popular literature and 'serious' literature viewed? Do these differ in the two periods?

3   What notion of 'cultural fall' informs the way Hoggart views the differences between the two periods?

Comments
1   One of the more innovative aspects of Hoggart's book is its examination of the relationship between popular entertainments and the daily, 'lived culture' of working people as manifested in their habits of language, views and attitudes, traditions of home and neighbourliness, and so on. However, Hoggart clearly views the relationship obtaining between these two areas of culture as different in the 1930s from those obtaining in the 1950s. In the case of the 1930s, the 'lived culture' of ordinary people is said to be, in a simple and direct way, reflected back to them in the books and stories they read. It is thus that he suggests that such BBC family serials as *The Archers* and *The Huggetts* 'simply present the people to the people' (p. 121) and describes the women's magazines of the period as, variously, having 'a felt sense of the texture of life in the group they cater for' (p. 121), reflecting 'the older forms of working-class life' (p. 122), as 'picture presentations of the known' (p. 128), and speaks of 'their extraordinary fidelity to the detail of readers' lives' (p. 126). Such forms, then, seem to grow organically out of the 'lived culture' of working people and to pull in the same direction, underlining and reinforcing it. The 'sex and violence' novels of the fifties, by contrast, lack any rootedness in the lived cultures of ordinary people. The values contained in them are represented as being entirely alien to the on-the-ground culture of working people and, via the reading habits of those groups who are temporarily dislocated from the support of their indigenous culture (such as young men in the armed services), as whittling away at the sturdier values inherited from an earlier phase in the class's history.

2   It is assumed, in both periods, that a fairly clear line separates popular literature from 'serious' literature. In the case of the 1930s, it is stated explicitly that we must not expect too much from the women's magazines of the period. Their scope and range is clearly limited. They are, nevertheless, defended on the grounds that 'they

may in all their triteness speak for a solid and relevant way of life' (p. 129). (It is also worth noting that Hoggart seems not to be aware of the extent to which, in endorsing reading matter for working-class women which affirms the values of home, family and marriage, his remarks could be regarded as both condescendingly middle-class *and* condescendingly sexist. A feminist reading of such magazines would be remarkably different!) The contrast between popular and serious reading is forged somewhat differently with regard to the literature of the 1950s. The sex-and-violence novels, it is admitted, do have a power and force of their own and exhibit certain stylistic similarities with the world of serious literature, as exemplified by Faulkner and Hemingway. The hard-hitting realism of the latter, however, is distinguished by the seriousness of the authors' moral or aesthetic intent. Popular writers drag the depths of life to no apparent purpose other than that of a cheap and vapid sensationalism.

3   Perhaps what most needs to be stressed, however, is the concept of cultural fall with which Hoggart operates. He is saying that once – in this case, the thirties – the culture of ordinary people, although not perfect, was not so bad but that since then it has taken a turn that is decidedly for the worse. It is this concept of cultural fall that links Hoggart decisively with the 'culture and civilization' tradition. What marks his particular position within that tradition, however, is that he places 'the world we have lost' not in some pre-industrial folk culture but in a particular phase in the development of working-class culture itself. As Gareth Stedman-Jones has argued, the working-class culture of the 1930s that serves Hoggart as his critical norm had its roots in the late nineteenth century, in the breakdown of an earlier, more separatist and politically orientated working-class culture (Stedman-Jones, 1974, p.93 in Reader 1). With the defeat of the Chartist movement and the subsequent 'creaming off' of a labour aristocracy – a stratum of skilled workers – from the working class as a whole, the former came increasingly to confine its political aspirations to goals realizable within capitalism and, in its culture, to incline increasingly towards forms that embodied some degree of acceptance of and accommodation with the economic and political status quo. It was a period when, rather than kicking against their class position, skilled workers settled into it, determined to make the best of a bad job by exploiting the economic and cultural space available to them to the full.

Although many of Hoggart's specific criticisms of the media are socialistically inclined, it is the fact that Hoggart contrasts the working-class culture of the present unfavourably with a highly idealized construction of a past and, moreover, politically quiescent phase in its development that connects his work with the predominantly conservative concerns of the 'culture and civilization' tradition. Yet, curiously, although the working-class culture of the 1930s, which serves as Hoggart's critical norm, had had its roots in the relatively deferential culture of the skilled sections of the working class in the late nineteenth century, the 'culture and civilization' tradition had first been formed in a reaction against precisely this period in the shaping of working-class culture. In order to appreciate why, it will repay our attention to consider the more important features which characterized the development of popular culture in the nineteenth century.

3   Theory of the history

It will be useful, here, to refer again to the problem, introduced in Units 1/2, of the historical range and application of the term 'popular culture'. If popular culture is held to consist of the entire range of cultural activities that take place outside the celebration of religious, civic or artistic values enshrined in the official or dominant culture, then, at least so far as societies for which we have written records are concerned, it would seem to have been a regular and recurring aspect of social life with an uninterrupted history running back to the Greeks. Further, if not exactly 'studied', the culture of the people has always been viewed as a matter for political concern, an area to be controlled and intervened in if necessary. Consisting of a wide range of often fiercely defended customs and rituals in which the people have defined and expressed themselves in ways contrary to those in which they have been defined or expressed within the official culture, the culture of the people has always been, at least in part, potentially subversive. And it has always drawn forth some combination of repression, alternative provision (the 'bread and circuses' tactic) or colonization, taking the sting out of the tail of subversive customs by assimilating them within the official culture. However, it was only with the formation of the 'culture and civilization' tradition in the nineteenth century that the culture of the people became, for the first time, a 'cultural' problem properly speaking, ushered forth in the newly provided clothes of 'mass culture' as the major culprit, both symptom and cause, of a decline within the very structure and fabric of civilization as a whole.

How is this qualitative development in the history of the theory of popular culture to be explained? I shall argue that it was, in part, a response to the equally dramatic shifts that took place within the sphere of popular culture itself. The transition from a predominantly agrarian to an industrialized capitalist society witnessed a shaking up of the cultural map, the like of which had not been seen before and, in this country, has not been seen since. It's not merely that traditional forms of popular recreation fell into disuse as the labouring population, moving from the countryside into the new industrial towns, responded, culturally, to the new rhythms of life and social relations imposed by an urban and industrial existence. Nor is it merely that this 'natural' process was greatly hastened by an industrializing bourgeoisie which waged a holy war on all popular pursuits which were felt to impede the formation of the new forms of work discipline required by industrial production. Nor, finally, was it simply a question of the development of new relations of cultural production (the mass media), capable of reaching into and defining the lives of working people in entirely new ways. What was involved was, above all, a reshaping of the entire field of cultural relationships between classes, the newer forms of popular culture occupying a position within that field which was different from that which had been occupied by the popular recreations of the past.

3.1 The eighteenth century

Parish wakes, the feasts of the Christian calendar, the seasonal festivities associated with agricultural life, pugilism, bull baiting, cock fighting, village football, a game of quoits at the local ale-house, village and country fairs with all the still familiar side-shows and competitions: these, according to Malcolmson (1973), comprised the vast bulk of the popular recreations of the common people during the eighteenth century. Several aspects of this list are worthy of note. The first is that , with the exception of the ale-houses – where the publican often acted as a commercial promoter on a small scale in order to attract trade – the degree of commercial penetration of such popular recreations was virtually zero. The majority of such pursuits were small-scale affairs, shaped in the system of social relationships prevailing at the local level.

Perhaps more important is the fact that, initially at any rate, these popular cultural pursuits did not add up to what could be described as a separate culture in the sense of being limited exclusively to artisans or agricultural workers. Blood sports and pugilism, in particular, were enthusiastically followed and sponsored by the landed gentry and aristocracy because of the opportunity they afforded for gambling and, more generally, the entire range of popular festivities and customs depended to a considerable extent on the patronage – or, at least, the tolerance – of local notables. Such patronage was partly the result of shared cultural tastes and interests; but it was equally, as both Malcolmson and E.P. Thompson have suggested, motivated by a concern for political and social stability. It formed, in fact, an integral aspect of a paternalist system and style of government, a unique blend of tolerance and enlightened self-interest, within which the cultural interests and tastes of the people were catered for from fear of the consequences that might otherwise follow – a truculent labour force and local unrest (see Thompson, 1974). And with good reason, for when towards the end of the century many popular recreations came under attack, the people proved capable of going to extreme lengths in their defence. However, this is to speak of later developments. For the greater part of the eighteenth century, the *dominant* picture is one of a popular cultural tradition that was not apart from or, in any developed sense, implacably opposed to the culture of the ruling classes but, to the contrary, of two cultures that interpenetrated, the cultural pursuits of the common people occupying a well defined, known and, on the whole, clearly subalterned position in relation to that of the landed classes. It was, that is to say, a culture that was 'placed'; a familiar component within an overall system of cultural relationships between classes that was, in part, anchored in traditional rights, expectations and reciprocal obligations.

Once this is said, however, it is important not to romanticize the cultural relationships of this period. There is some truth in Henry Fielding's portrayal, in the figure of Squire Western in *Tom Jones*, of the gentry of England as a bibulous and gout-ridden squirarchy locked in boozy harmony with the rough, unpolished rustic culture of the people. But it is only a partial truth. Towards the end of the century, the aristocracy and the upper sections of the middle class began to withdraw their patronage from the sphere of popular recreations and to cultivate increasingly class-specific leisure pursuits. The importance of the London season and the growth of the spa towns attested to a class that was more interested in exclusive social intercourse within its own boundaries than with traditional patterns of cross-class recreation. Furthermore, the recreations of the common people were a matter of public concern throughout the century. This was, in part, a reflection of the sheer robustness of many popular recreations and of the drunkenness, bawdiness and licentiousness that frequently accompanied them. This, of course, had always been the grounds for Puritan opposition to the culture of the common people and, throughout the century, as E.P. Thompson has put it, 'the breaking loose of this hell of a plebeian culture quite beyond their control was the waking nightmare of the surviving Puritans' (Thompson, 1974, p. 395). If it is a normative concern with the culture of the people that one is looking for, it is the muted voice of eighteenth-century Puritanism that provides it as popular recreations were routinely and roundly condemned for their morally corrupting influence, their undermining of the habits of sobriety and, perhaps most sustainedly, for their violation of the sabbath. The attitude of the predominantly Anglican gentry and magistracy was quite different. Viewing such excesses as a necessary safety valve, they intervened only – although not infrequently – when the vigour of such popular recreations posed a threat to civic order or private property.

The concerns expressed in relation to the culture of the common people were thus predominantly *political* concerns and not *cultural* ones, for the dividing line between the 'boisterous folk' and the political mob was a thin one and frequently crossed. Many popular recreations – village football in particular – constituted a demonstration of the people's power, a taking over of public space which involved an often quite open cowing and intimidation of the respectable citizenry. More importantly, however, popular sports often spilt over into forms of collective behaviour that were more directly and palpably political. Malcolmson, reporting an account from the *Northampton Mercury* of 1765 to the effect that a crowd having assembled at West-Haddon, ostensibly in order to play football, 'soon after meeting formed themselves into a tumultuous Mob, and pulled up and burnt the Fences designed for the Inclosure of that Field, and did other considerable Damage', thus concludes that football 'was a convenient and sometimes effective pretence for gathering together a large assemblage of local dissidents; and it could only have functioned in this way, as a convincing shield for rebellious intentions, if it were a familiar, accepted, and relatively ordinary reason for drawing together a considerable crowd' (Malcolmson, 1973, p.40).

This tendency for popular recreations to take on a proto-political aspect increased as the century developed. Edward Thompson's essays on 'Patrician society, plebeian culture' and 'Eighteenth-century English society: class struggle without class?' are instructive in this respect. They remind us that the culture of the common people in the eighteenth century was not the traditional culture of a peasantry but a distinctively new cultural formation – a 'plebeian culture'. Its basis was provided by skilled artisans and agricultural labourers caught up in not feudal, but capitalist social relationships which afforded them a considerable degree of independence from the direct control, supervision and cultural influence of their employers. And, as Thompson insists, this 'plebeian culture' was by no means a tamed or deferential one. While it may have occupied a settled and defined place within what Thompson refers to as the 'field of force' governed by the cultural dominance of the gentry (Thompson, 1978, p.154), it was relatively unaffected in its character by either the religious or secular ideologies of the ruling classes. It was, moreover, a spontaneously rebellious culture but, as Thompson puts it, 'rebellious in defence of tradition' (Thompson, 1978, p.154). It is clear that, in speaking of 'culture' here, Thompson has in mind the distinctive political culture of the common people as much as their recreations. The important point, however, is to grasp the interpenetration of the two. Popular recreations, as we have seen , frequently served as the cover or recruiting ground for popular political action.

Equally, popular unrest – and it is in this respect that Thompson refers to the culture as being 'rebellious in defence of tradition' – was usually directed at projected encroachments on the people's traditional rights and customs: the enclosure of common land, the departure from traditional methods for fixing the price of bread and, equally centrally, the attempted regulation or prohibition of popular recreations themselves. The two were inseparably clasped, part of an overall culture of protest that expressed itself in local acts of defiance, riot and, in some cases, sedition.

It is small wonder then that, in the eighteenth century, the people were often regarded as 'ungovernable'. Yet, for the greater part, such rebelliousness was contained within clearly defined limits. The Whig aristocracy may have 'loathed the licentious crowd' (Thompson, 1978, p.145) and have sought every opportunity to curb its excesses but, by and large, the dominance of the landed aristocracy remained unchallenged. Directly coercive means for imposing the will of the dominant classes existed. Indeed, in some respects, especially in regard to the laws concerning matters such as theft or poaching, coercion formed a part of the regular system of relations between rulers and ruled. For the greater part, however, the myriad local acts of disobedience and rebellion did not amount to a movement which seriously challenged either the power or legitimacy of the state. At this level, government was by consent, based on the passive acquiescence if not the enthusiastic support of the majority of the population. As Thompson concludes:

> This plebeian culture was not, to be sure, a revolutionary nor even a proto-revolutionary culture (in the sense of fostering ulterior objectives which called in question the social order); but one should not describe it as a deferential culture either. It bred riots but not rebellions: direct actions but not democratic organizations.
>
> (Thompson, 1974, p.397)

The formative working-class culture of the first half of the nineteenth century, by contrast, bred both rebellions and democratic organizations, the combination producing a crisis of social authority that was as deep as it was prolonged.

3.2 The nineteenth century

Obviously, there is no magic line separating the eighteenth from the nineteenth century. The forces bearing upon the transformation of eighteenth century plebeian culture had their roots in the 1760s, gradually picked up momentum as the century progressed and gave way to the new one to yield, by the mid-nineteenth century, a system of cultural relationships between classes that had been thoroughly transformed. It is also clear that these changes in the sphere of culture and ideology were not isolated developments. They formed merely a part of a whole complex of processes bearing upon the transformation of the economy from a predominantly agrarian to an increasingly industrialized form of capitalism. In what follows, I can deal only with those forces bearing most directly on the reshaping of the culture of the common people, modifying its distinctive forms and content and, above all, shifting its position, its 'place', within the system of cultural relationships as a whole.

Clearly the structural changes associated with the shift to an increasingly urban and industrialized economy had a significant bearing on popular recreations. The seasonal celebrations associated with rural life obviously had little meaning in an urban environment and tended, in part, to fall 'naturally' into disuse. Equally, the overcrowded, unplanned industrial towns afforded little communal space within which the more robust forms of the earlier plebeian culture might be accommodated with the result that these, where they survived, tended to be more limited and confined. The other side of the picture, of course, consists in the new cultural forms constructed within the milieu of the formative working class in response to the new conditions of existence imposed by industrial and urban life. The genesis of industrial folk song was particularly important in this respect, reflecting, as A.L. Lloyd put it, 'the life and aspirations of a raw class in the making, of men handling new-fashioned tools, thinking new thoughts, standing in novel relationship to each other and to their masters' (Lloyd, 1975, p.297).

Perhaps the most important consequence of structural change, however, was the sheer physical separation of classes to which it gave rise. The social geography of the new industrial town was characterized by a clear split between residential districts: the working population huddled in back-to-back terraces and hovels on one side of town and the mansions of the bourgeoisie on the other. This geographical separation was reinforced by the social relations of the workplace. The new factory worker typically knew his employer by name only whereas, for the factory owner, his employees were just so many 'hands', anonymous and interchangeable. There thus opened up, across this physical and geographical separation of classes, a cultural divide: a perception of 'two nations' whose ways, manners and customs were, to a degree, alien and unknown to one another.

The creation of this physical gulf between class cultures is crucial. It meant that the culture, in all senses of the word – the habits and customs defining their 'way of life'; their distinctive songs; their reading matter – of the first two generations of the urban working class developed within a cultural space that was visibly and dramatically separated from that of the ruling classes. The conduits between the culture and ideology of the dominant classes and those of the common people had been broken, except for the odd missionary outpost and the local constabulary.

However, neither the decline of earlier forms of popular recreation nor the creation of this cultural rift between classes can be viewed solely or even mainly as the result of changes within the structure of the economy. Thompson takes this line of argument sternly to task in *The Making of the English Working Class*, showing that the traditional pastimes of the people did not so much 'decline' but were rather hounded out of existence. This was, it is true, partly the result of direct economic pressures as land that had previously been set aside or, by tradition, claimed for popular recreations was suddenly at a premium and, in the face of much popular opposition, forcibly taken over and devoted to other purposes – sheep farming in the countryside, for example, or building in the newly developing towns. More important, however, were the ideological pressures dictated by the need to transform an agricultural population, bred on a robust and rebellious culture, into a sober and orderly workforce subjugated to the rigours and discipline of factory production. The last quarter of the eighteenth century and the first half of the nineteenth century witnessed both the withdrawal of the patronage and tolerance of the gentry and an unprecedented assault on the entire range of popular recreations. Moral crusaders inveighed against fairs and carnivals on the grounds of their immorality and godlessness; against public holidays on the grounds that they were too numerous and undermined work discipline; against the violence, excesses and corrupting influence of blood sports. The local magistracy intervened to prohibit those popular sports that tended to result in public disorder; the licensing laws were used to curb the promotional activities of ale-houses. Parliament lent its support by outlawing many forms of popular recreation: new gaming laws severely restricted the people's rights of access to and usage of the countryside; the Cruelty to Animals Act of 1835 made all popular blood sports illegal except, significantly enough, those of the aristocracy and *haute bourgeoisie*.

It would be a mistake to exaggerate the effectiveness of these measures. Many traditional pursuits survived in a variety of illegal or semi-clandestine forms. Moreover, according to Hugh Cunningham, the popular culture of the first half of the nineteenth century was extraordinarily vigorous, a period of major expansion for fairs, prize-fighting and wrestling, all of which survived the withdrawal of the patronage of the wealthy, as well as a period in which new forms of popular culture – notably the circus and melodrama – made their first appearance (see Cunningham, 1980, Chapter 1). Nor would it be correct to view the ruling classes as speaking with one voice on these matters. Tory opinion, in particular, was divided with many prominent Tories siding with the people and arguing for the revival of older forms of patronage and against the reforming zeal of liberals, radicals and evangelists of all kinds. Nonetheless, the predominant current ran in the opposite direction.

The system of cultural relationships which had typified the eighteenth century, then, did not change of its own accord in response to the supposedly neutral requirements of 'industrialization'. Rather, it was actively dismantled from 'above' by an industrializing bourgeoisie acting, sometimes in conflict, sometimes in unison, with a landed gentry bent on an increasingly rationalized and profitable use of land. This onslaught was complemented by an attempted 'cultural penetration of the poor', an attempt to infiltrate the increasingly separate culture of the people and to influence its development. To understand the form that this attempted cultural penetration took, it is necessary to appreciate the failure of the Anglican Church to retain any appreciable grip on the cultural lives of the common people. This failure had already been manifest in the eighteenth century. Malcolmson notes the tendency, as the century developed, for the truly popular feasts and festivals to be those associated with the seasonal rhythms of the agricultural year as opposed to those officially celebrated in the Christian calendar, a fact that lead Thompson to conclude that 'the Church lost command over the "leisure" of the poor, their feasts and festivals, and, with this, over a large area of plebeian culture' (Thompson, 1974, p.391). This deficiency was highlighted in the nineteenth century as the established Church – its clergy still predominantly recruited from the gentry – proved totally incapable of making any appreciable headway in the new industrial towns: Foster records that, in Oldham in 1821, the Anglican churches could claim a combined congregation of only 400 regular communicants out of a population of 38,000 (see Foster, 1974, p.29).

The period from the 1790s onward witnessed an attempt by a wide variety of voluntary or benevolent organizations to fill the gap left by the established Church. In part, such initiatives came from within the Anglican Church as a result of the increasing influence of Evangelism. Hannah More and the Sunday School Movement, Bishop Barrington's Society for Bettering the Conditions of the Poor, William Wilberforce and John Bowdler's Society for the Suppression of Vice and Encouragement of Religion and, later, the Society for the Promotion of Christian Knowledge are examples. For the greater part, however, these remained marginal to the life of the majority of the newly urbanized working class. But Methodism, the most influential form of non-conformism, did not. Yet its legacy was ambivalent: as Thompson argues, it injected into working-class communities not merely religion but also literacy and a tradition of self-education and self-organization that was to play a major part in the political education of the working class when, in the years of the Napoleonic Wars, radicalism was pushed underground.

This raises the final consideration with which we need to concern ourselves at this point: the fact that the structural factors making for the separation of the culture of the working class in the process of its formation were compounded by this culture being *pushed* into separation, isolation, secrecy and self-reliance by the punitive measures taken by the government to quell the rising tide of radicalism and, later, trade unionism. Here, again, we can only nibble at the edges of a long and complicated history whose central contours were moulded by the French Revolution and the Napoleonic Wars, and whose result was the re-articulation of political divisions along lines that were more clearly class-based than they had been in the eighteenth century.

Initially an adjunct of Tory and Whig radicalism, the tradition of political radicalism nurtured in the artisan occupations of the eighteenth century was forced into independence in the 1790s as both Tories and Whigs, fearful at the revolutionary turn taken by events in France, turned tail on their earlier radical aspirations and supported Pitt's attempts to construct a 'fortress Britain', armed with a battery of repressive measures – sedition laws, laws governing public assemblies, the taxation of the press – as much against sedition and rebellion at home as against the threat of foreign invasion. Yet the results of these measures were, in some senses, the opposite of those intended. For the culture of protest did not wither or languish so much as simply go underground with the result that the common people of England responded, politically, to the experience of their proletarianization in a way that was profoundly hidden from the view of the dominant classes. The radical culture that had been inherited from the eighteenth century continued to be nurtured in a variety of illegal and secret organizations, was circulated effectively on a mass basis by a highly efficient radical press and, to the extent that the connections that had hitherto subordinated it to Tory or Whig leadership had been severed, was developed in a direction that was increasingly distinctively working class in both organizational form and political content.

The instant dramatic success of Thomas Paine's *Rights of Man* – it sold 50,000 copies within a few weeks of its first publication in 1791 – was sufficient testimony to a broadly-based popular radicalism which, in aspiration at least, aimed at the refounding of the social order, from top to bottom.

14

3.3 New lines of settlement

It can be seen from the above that the cultural consequences of the formation of an industrialized form of capitalism were not limited to altering the *forms* and *content* of the culture of the common people. It is not merely that the 'plebeian culture' of the eighteenth century became the 'working class culture' of the early nineteenth century. The processes that wrought this transition simultaneously altered the 'place' that the culture of ordinary people occupied within the culture of the whole. In early modern Europe, Peter Burke has argued, 'popular culture was everyone's culture; a second culture for the educated, and the only culture for everyone else'. By the nineteenth century, however, the ruling classes 'had abandoned popular culture to the lower classes, from whom they were now separated, as never before, by profound differences in world-view' (Burke, 1978, p.270).

Note should also be taken of the weakening of traditional forms of social authority associated with these transformations. The years of the Napoleonic Wars witnessed the widespread and routine suppression of an illegal tradition of radicalism that continued to smoulder, unabated, within the increasingly separate and separated culture of the formative working class. In the late 1830s and 1840s, this radicalism broke cover and, in the form of the distinctively working-class political demands embodied in the Chartist programme (most notably, the demand for universal suffrage so that Parliament might be used to control capitalism in the interests of the working classes) challenged, if not the ability, then at least the right of the ruling classes to govern. Although by no means the full story, the cultural divide that had opened up between classes stood as both major symptom and chief cause of this malady. The culture of the people was no longer subalterned to that of the dominant classes, was no longer held in place beneath it, but developed in its own, separate space, seemingly impenetrable; it stood outside and was, in part, resolutely opposed to the ruling class ideology.

Yet by the 1870s the situation had changed dramatically as new lines of cultural settlement were installed which, with minor modifications, were to last until the end of the Great War. Again, structural factors must be allowed their part. Although the Great Depression of the 1880s and early 1890s gave rise to widespread social unrest, especially on the part of the casual poor and unemployed of the London dockland areas, and although by the 1890s the declining competitiveness of English manufacturing industries in relation to those of Germany and America signalled the end of her industrial pre-eminence, the effects of these developments were somewhat offset by an aggressive policy of imperialist expansion. Although, of course, unevenly distributed, there is little doubt that real earnings rose significantly during the last quarter of the century: Hobsbawm estimates that average real wages increased by a third between 1875 and 1900 (Hobsbawm, 1969, p.160). Cheap consumer goods, an improving diet, a longer life expectancy, reduced infantile mortality rates; in these and a host of related ways the *employed* sections of the working classes acquired a real, material stake in the well-being of capitalism.

The growing complexity of new forms of industrial organization entailed by an increasingly sophisticated technology also played its part. It resulted, as John Foster and Robert Gray have argued in, respectively, *Class Struggle and the Industrial Revolution* and *The Labour Aristocracy in Victorian Edinburgh*, in an increasingly pronounced internal differentiation of the working class as highly skilled and supervisory workers were creamed off from the class at large and incorporated into the dominant culture – partly by increased monetary rewards but, more sustainedly, by being offered a place within the new liberal ideology of progress, and an identity as subjects of the world's foremost imperialist power. This is not to suggest that the 'labour aristocracy' (a concept as controversial as the thesis of which it forms a part) entirely abandoned earlier traditions of political radicalism. The records show that skilled workers were to the forefront in many of the political and industrial disputes of the period. The point is rather that, in aiming to improve the political and economic position of the working classes *within* capitalism, such struggles reflected a degree of ideological accommodation with capitalism which, although by no means total, was greater than that which prevailed during the heyday of Chartist agitation.

An important part of this process was the increased *privatization* of leisure in the nineteenth century. In pre-industrial Britain, popular recreations tended either to be centred on the place of work or to take place in open, public and communal spaces: the village common, for instance. By the end of the eighteenth century, Hugh Cunningham records, such public spaces were being appropriated increasingly by the wealthy for their own, exclusive private use. At the same time, the upper classes tended to retreat from the public sphere of shared recreations into the home as the new, preferred location for their leisure pursuits – a pattern that was followed by the middle classes in the nineteenth century. This, in turn, entailed that the common people, forced to find new locations for their recreations, turned increasingly to the public house – a 'closed' space, inaccessible to members of the governing classes. This process, Cunningham concludes, 'entailed for all classes a privatization of leisure, privatization in the sense that leisure became class-bound and impenetrable for those outside the class in question' (Cunningham, 1980, p.76). By the mid-nineteenth century, the middle classes, alarmed at this process leading to the increased separation of the classes, sought to counteract it by creating a new kind of public leisure space – paid for out of the public purse – in order that working-class leisure might be more visible and more easily controlled. It is thus notable that the last quarter of the century witnessed the provision of a plethora of state provided locations for popular recreations – public parks, libraries, museums – which aimed at promoting leisure of a 'rational' and improving kind. However, the same period also witnessed a tendency for the home to become a centre for working-class leisure; the home as a centre of domesticity, of values of family life that were highly congenial to the middle classes and which were cultivated in a massive, 'improving' literature directed at the working class, particularly at the working-class wife and mother. The result of these combined tendencies was that, by the end of the nineteenth century, working-class leisure had been massively re-located, situated increasingly in the home as a site of middle-class influenced values, in the new public spaces provided by the state, in work-based leisure pursuits subjected to the influence and patronage of employers and, of course, in a vastly expanded sphere of commercially provided places of recreation.

This raises, as a more general matter, the new strategies and forms for the 'cultural penetration of the poor' that were developed from the mid-nineteenth century onward. The activities of benevolent organizations continued, of course, often taking new forms. There was, however, an increasing perception that the scope of the problem exceeded the ambit of voluntary and benevolent organizations and required the intervention of the state.

From the days of Jacobin radicalism up to the years of Chartist revolt, the state had intervened in the culture of the working classes by and large negatively, seeking to restrict it by hemming it in within a finely meshed network of legal prohibitions and restrictions. The latter half of the century, by contrast, witnessed the cessation of legal prohibitions, yielding a 'free market' in the sphere of culture, counterbalanced by the state's adoption of a more actively interventionist policy of cultural penetration. With regard to the latter, the increased provision of public education was by far the most important development. Popular instruction had, of course, been provided before, but it was now provided in a new way with markedly new political and cultural implications. Richard Johnson has written instructively on this subject, pointing to the existence of a widespread, albeit institutionally fragile, tradition of radical schooling and self-education within the working class, a tradition that was highly critical of and strenuously resisted attempts to impose alternative forms of educational provision from outside the class (Johnson, 1979). Such attempts were originally made by voluntary organizations – the Mechanics' Institutes, the Society for the Diffusion of Useful Knowledge, founded in the 1830s – whose endeavours were often ridiculed and lampooned as too palpably seeking to offer not instruction in political and practical matters that would be useful to working-class pupils but, as it was satirized by Cobbett, 'Heddekeshun': alien types of knowledge and hierarchical relationships of educational authority that were viewed, in the radical press, as bourgeois in both form and inspiration. This hostility towards and suspicion of the provisions of voluntary organizations was subsequently transferred to state provided educational schemes. Of course, this is not to speak against such provision. It is merely to point out that the state's initial ventures into the sphere of education took place in a particular historical context, its provision of popular schooling forming a conduit along which there passed – and was seen to pass – not merely instruction, in a neutral sense, but the formative ideologies of liberalism and imperialism and new forms of social discipline.

Critically important though these developments were, their significance was eclipsed by the development of commercial forms of cultural penetration. The formation of the popular press and the creation of a separate market for popular fiction directed at a specifically working-class readership were the earliest and perhaps the most significant developments in this respect. I have remarked earlier that the first half of the century witnessed the development of a radical press which – in spite of legal prohibitions – was widely circulated and read throughout the working class. By the late 1860s, this circulation had fallen off dramatically and the number of papers and periodicals had been significantly reduced. James Curran has suggested that this was chiefly because of the creation of a 'free market' in publishing in the 1850s (see Curran, 1977). During the Napoleonic Wars, an attempt had been made to price the radical press out of existence by the imposition of a tax on advertising and a stamp duty on the cost of paper. These two duties were removed in 1853 and 1855 respectively, with the effect of dramatically reducing the size of the radical press as a result of the logic of the 'free market'. For the repeal of the duties enabled the capitalist press to reduce prices below the cost of production (largely because of the significantly increased advertising revenue it attracted) at a time when, as a result of technological developments, costs of production and capital requirements were rising way beyond the means of independent radical publishers. In the ensuing price war, the radical press was routed.

The popular press that installed itself in the place previously occupied by the radical press – the forerunners of today's Sunday newspapers – significantly modified the cultural diet of the literate members of the working class. Indeed, it constituted perhaps the single most important instrument of ideological penetration, injecting into working-class homes, pubs and coffee houses 'values and perspectives. . . at total variance with those mediated by early radical newspapers' (Curran, 1977, pp.222–23).

The history of book publishing followed a similar trajectory. Whereas the working class had initially expended its literacy on literature of a political or self-improving kind, there being scarcely any identifiable split between middle-class and working-class markets, the period from the 1830s witnessed the formation of a separate market for the working-class reading public and the development of new forms of popular fiction – usually plagiarized and bowdlerized forms of the middle-class novel – which were circulated through the class by new systems of distribution. In *Fiction for the Working Man*, the classic work on the subject, Louis James refers to the 1830s as a decade in which the working class was led 'from politics to fiction'; increasingly to experience and respond to its situation through the mediation of fictional forms that were provided for it by penny-a-liners working to the formulaic requirements of mass publishing on a commercial basis.

Although providing its most obvious instance, commercial penetration of the sphere of working-class culture was not confined to the press and publishing. Indeed, on all fronts, working-class cultural forms and activities were reached into, modified and redefined by increasingly sophisticated forms of commercial entertainment. The drink trade was significantly reorganized and expanded; Tin Pan Alley was born as the commercial song vied with, transformed and co-opted earlier traditions of working-class song; the music hall became a minor industry – the forerunner of today's 'showbiz' and, as Gareth Stedman-Jones has argued, a major forum for the dissemination of imperialist rhetoric and of an over-sentimentalized view of working-class life, a form in which the class viewed itself through the cracked looking-glass of its own caricaturization (Stedman-Jones, 1974, p.108–18 in Reader 1).

So far as Hugh Cunningham is concerned, he is in little doubt that the commercialization of popular culture was of decisive political significance:

> The strength of popular demand was such that many direct efforts to control leisure failed, yet that demand was contained within a world of commercialized leisure which provided its own controls. From the point of view of authority this commercialized leisure was increasingly acceptable, for if what was offered within it was hardly uplifting, at least it posed no threat. On the contrary, leisure was shorn of many of its political and social associations,

and while the way it was spent might be individually damaging, it was no longer politically or socially dangerous.
(Cunningham, 1980, p.141)

To conclude, then, there developed in the latter half of the nineteenth century distinctively new means and forms of the 'cultural penetration of the poor'. It would be mistaken to view these as the product of a ruling-class conspiracy. The state, benevolent organizations, the press and the developing entertainment industries often pulled in contradictory directions: the temperance movement indicted the brewing industry, educational reformers regretted the morally corrupting influences of the popular press, and so on. But it is clear that, taken collectively, these different initiatives did add up to a significantly new system for the regulation of the cultural relationships between classes, new ways of pinning down the culture of working people, defining the space available to it and holding it in place beneath the dominant culture. Yet, having said that, it needs to be acknowledged that the cultural penetration achieved in these ways was always less than complete. It rarely reached beyond the upper strata of skilled and respectable workers beyond which, as Gareth Stedman-Jones has shown in *Outcast London*, there remained the vast reaches of the unskilled and casual poor and, of course, the unemployed. These, the 'dangerous classes', remained permanently on the other side of a cultural divide, a *terra incognita* whose presence continued to haunt the dark underside of the bourgeoisie's consciousness: a visible refutation of the liberal ideology of progress and, when mobilized in industrial or political action, a real threat to the apparent calm Victorian England.

You should now try to pull together the argument developed in Section 3 of this unit by summarizing the more important changes that characterized the development of popular culture in the nineteenth century. Go through each of the three periods I have discussed picking out what you consider to be their key characteristics, paying particular attention to the differences in the relationships between classes which the popular cultures of the three periods attest to.

Comment   The most important change I have been trying to put across concerns the ways in which the culture of ordinary people was subject to influence and regulation from 'above'. Clearly, the nineteenth century witnessed a massive shift in the *content* of popular culture: from bull baiting and cock fighting to the music hall and organized sport. By the end of the nineteenth century we can speak of an industrial working class both producing and consuming forms of popular culture that are recognizably continuous with those we know today. This shift in the *content* of popular culture, however, was also accompanied and, in part, brought about by related changes in the *forms* through which the cultural relationships between the dominant and subordinate classes were *structured*. In the eighteenth century, the dominant classes influenced popular recreations largely through the operation of private patronage. By the mid-nineteenth century, such lines of influence and control had been largely severed resulting in a degree of separation of working-class culture from ruling-class control, which accompanied and was, in part, viewed as contributing to its political radicalization as manifested in the history of the Chartist movement. By the end of the nineteenth century, new *forms* of control – principally commercial and state provided – had been built across the cultural divide that had separated the classes in mid-century. These new forms of control, I have argued, played an important role in shaping the predominantly *reformist*, rather than *revolutionary*, political orientation of the working class. Apart from pre-figuring the twentieth century in terms of the *content* of popular culture, the forms of cross-class influence and control developed by the late nineteenth century also point to our own century, during which both commercial and state provided forms of popular culture – I am thinking especially of broadcasting – have expanded dramatically.

18

4 History of the theory

4.1 The crisis of culture

The foregoing historical detour has been necessary in order to contextualize adequately the ideological and political concerns that were worked through within the 'culture and civilization' tradition. For these were a response, not so much to changes in the form and content of the culture of the people, as to what was perceived as the disintegration of a hitherto harmoniously ordered set of cultural relationships between classes, which the new forms of popular culture served merely to symbolize. Furthermore, although the distinctive concerns of this tradition were developed in a discourse organized centrally on the concept of culture, far more than culture was at stake. The real issue, as Leavis put it, was that of 'the standard of living'. Culture critique, that is to say, was a form of political and social commentary in which social ills were diagnosed by means of their cultural symptoms. But these symptoms were also viewed as the points to which remedial action would need to be applied if the plight of culture – and, with it, that of civilization and society – was to be ameliorated. Tracing the disintegrative effects of industrial capitalism as they manifested themselves in the sphere of culture, the 'culture and civilization' tradition girded itself to combat these not by political means but by cultural ones.

The development of such an integrative, synthesizing body of theory organized around the concept of culture was a significantly new departure in the history of social thought. While the development of the novel in the eighteenth century had given rise to a concern with the standards of 'culture', particularly with regard to how these might be maintained in face of the increasing penetration of the sphere of culture by market relationships, these 'cultural' concerns were not linked with political ones. The price of novels and the social distribution of literacy in the eighteenth century meant that the novel-reading public was a fairly restricted one, virtually exclusively middle class, and the terms of the cultural debate inaugurated by the novel were, accordingly, drawn with reference solely to this class. It was not the culture of the people and its effects upon the whole that was at issue, but the consequences for the culture of the 'cultured' of organizing cultural production on a commodity basis. As I have noted, the culture of the common people had been viewed as a matter for *political* concern in the eighteenth century. But it was not regarded as either particularly worthy of or in need of study, and it certainly did not figure within any integrative body of theory about culture as a whole and its bearing on 'the standard of living'.

Indeed, as Peter Burke has argued, one cannot speak of a serious or developed intellectual interest in the cultural pursuits of ordinary people prior to the romantic discovery of the 'folk' in Germany towards the end of the eighteenth century (see Burke, 1978, Chapter 1). The works of Goethe and of Johann Gottfried Herder were especially influential in this respect, constructing a highly idealized image of the traditional, pre-industrial 'folk' which, transposed into England via the work of Thomas Carlyle, was to serve as a normative standard against which the cultural consequences of industrial capitalism were to be judged and found wanting by the early Victorian Romantics. In *Culture and Society,* Raymond Williams has charted the influence of the Romantic critique on the subsequent development of nineteenth century thought. He shows how its presence continued to be felt within the mainline of the 'culture and civilization' tradition, explaining much of the ambivalence of this tradition in articulating a complex mixture of conservative yet, at the same time, anti-capitalist sentiments. He also shows how, from the other direction as it were, the embryonically socialist criticisms of such continuators of the Romantic tradition as William Morris and John Ruskin were influenced by the perspectives of the more straightforward conservatively inclined strands of the 'culture and civilization' tradition.

Bearing this important qualification in mind, the most distinctive characteristic of the period was such that, by the end of the century, the 'folk' favoured by the Romantics had become the 'masses'. The culture of the 'non-cultured', from being a critical norm, had become an index of cultural decline. Inserted within a new system of oppositions – mass versus folk, high versus low, élite versus mass – it became the major stamping-ground on which the social and political criticisms of a predominantly conservatively inclined tradition of cultural pessimism were rehearsed. Whereas in the eighteenth century the concern about the standard of culture was articulated largely in relation to the nascent culture of the middle class, while the culture of the common people had figured largely as a matter for political concern, the distinctiveness of the 'culture and civilization' tradition is marked by its bringing together *both* political *and* cultural concerns in and around a concern with the culture of the common people.

The central problem that was addressed within this tradition, albeit obliquely, was the problem of *social order,* in which the culture of the common people was interpreted as evidence of a serious weakening of traditional forms of social authority. Matthew Arnold communicates this apprehension in his description of the 'Hyde Park rough', his indirect way of referring to working-class political protest:

> He has no visionary schemes of revolution and transformation, though of course he would like his class to rule, as the aristocratic class like their class to rule, and the middle class theirs. But meanwhile our social machine is a little out of order; there are a good many people in our paradisiacal centres of industrialism and individualism taking the bread out of one another's mouths. The rough has not yet quite found his groove and settled down to his work, and so he is just asserting his personal liberty a little, going where he likes, assembling where he likes, bawling as he likes, hustling as he likes. Just as the rest of us, – as the country squires in the aristocratic class, as the political dissenters in the middle class, – he has no idea of a *State,* of the nation in its collective and corporate character controlling, as government, the free swing of this or that one of its members in the name of the higher reason of all of them, his own as well as that of others.
>
> (Arnold, 1971, p.65)

Culture and Anarchy was first published in 1869 and it bristles with allusions to the political tensions that had characterized the preceding five years: the widespread popular protest accompanying the progress of the 1867 Reform Bill, serious disturbances in Ireland, an agricultural crisis creating unrest in the countryside, insurrection in Jamaica and, following the death of Viscount Palmerston, the Prime Minister, in 1865, the renewal of hostilities between commercial and landed interests. Arnold's fear of anarchy was not the product of idle rumination on the abstracted problem of culture, and he was quite unequivocal in declaring that, when and where necessary, this threat should be countered by the use of directly coercive means. The need that he articulated, however, was for the formation of a 'centre of authority', embodied in the state, that would reduce such occasions to a minimum by producing, within the members of all classes, a voluntary compliance with the direction given to social and political life by the representatives of such a 'centre of authority'.

We can see, here, how Arnold responded to a political problem – that of disorder – by redefining it as a cultural problem. If anarchy threatens, it is because the mechanisms of culture have broken down with the result that different classes pursue their own interests rather than subordinate them to a consensually agreed upon 'centre of authority'. How was such a 'centre of authority' to be created? Arnold's proposals here were somewhat vague and contradictory, but central to them was the dissemination of the standards of 'culture' – of 'the best that has been thought and known in the world' – throughout all classes by means of public education. But it had to be *real* culture:

> Plenty of people will try to give the masses, as they call them, an intellectual food prepared and adapted in the way they think proper for the actual condition of the masses. The ordinary popular literature is an example of this way of working on the masses . . . but culture works differently. It does not try to teach down to the level of the inferior masses; it does not try to win them for this or that sect of its own, with ready-made judgements and watchwords. It seeks to do away with classes; to make the best that has been thought and known in the world current everywhere . . .
>
> (Arnold, 1971, p.56)

This concern with culture – with 'real culture' – is central to an understanding of the 'culture and civilization' tradition. For this embodied not merely a conservative response to the ideological, cultural and political development of the working class. It was also, and more particularly, a critique of the 'new lines of settlement' forged by, among other things, the development of commercial forms of popular culture. These were viewed critically partly because the social cohesion they produced was regarded as insufficient and unstable, unable to ward off the threat of disorder inasmuch as they tended to produce a numbing of the mind rather than any generally shared set of values which could be subscribed to genuinely by the members of all classes. Yet they were also condemned on the grounds that, to the extent that they did achieve social cohesion, they did so at the price of sacrificing culture. In this respect, the Romantic critique of industrial capitalism was redeployed in a political-cum-cultural critique of the new industrial bourgeoisie. Indicted for its vulgarity and philistinism, it was also brought to court for its failure to serve as an adequate 'centre of authority': hence the argument of Arnold and others that the state should step in to fill this gap.

Although so far I have dealt solely with developments in Britain, these should not be seen in isolation. The 'culture and civilization' tradition constituted by the line running from Arnold to Leavis and Eliot is but the local branch of a more general theoretical tendency which, in the late nineteenth century, was developed in western Europe and which, since the 1930s, has also exerted a powerful influence in the United States. I refer here to what is customarily known as the 'mass society' or 'élite' tradition of social theory: to the work of Friedrich Nietzsche in Germany, of Gaetano Mosca and Vilfredo Pareto in Italy and, although somewhat later, of Ortega y Gasset in Spain. According to these theorists, the political and cultural enfranchisement of the common people, effected by the development of political democracy and the spread of literacy associated with the development of the popular press, had tended to undermine a supposedly natural distinction between the 'masses' and society's élites – political and cultural – with the result that cultural standards were lowered and political stability threatened. However, it would be wrong to suggest that, either in this country or in Europe, the concerns expressed in these traditions resulted in a study of the new forms of 'mass culture' of a detailed or empirical kind. This did not occur until the 1930s – chiefly by Leavis and his associates in this country and, in the United States, by the first generation of American sociologists. Yet, in both cases, the terms of reference within which such studies were located were supplied by the inherited and revivified traditions of late nineteenth-century social and cultural theory. As a consequence of the dominance of these traditions, the study of popular culture has, until recently, largely taken the form of a 'mass culture' critique. Viewed as both symptom and cause of a deep-seated cultural malaise penetrating all spheres of social life, its analysis has been a means of articulating a web of intersecting anxieties concerning the political, cultural and ideological consequences of the development of capitalism, the extension of the franchise and the development of those new forms of cultural production – the press, film, radio and television – customarily referred to as the mass media.

In spite of the predominance of such concerns, however, it would be misleading to suggest that the work of such cultural pessimists has constituted the only source of our knowledge about popular culture. Account must also be taken of the work of historians and, perhaps more particularly, of ethnographers, especially with regard to the study of the popular customs and rituals – the culture 'as a whole way of life' – of different sections of the community. For these have yielded, at an empirical level, a body of detailed knowledge of such popular customs which has been produced at a remove from the governing concerns of the 'culture and civilization' tradition. Mention must also be made of Mass Observation, a movement founded by Tom Harrison and Charles Madge in the 1930s. The product of a general 'need to know' about the culture of ordinary people that manifested itself, on other fronts, in the documentary film movement of Humphrey Jennings and John Grierson and the development of public opinion polls, the ambition of Mass Observation was to found an objective science of the people, to interpret the people to themselves and to the government of the day, to bridge the gap of ignorance that had opened up between class cultures, between rulers and ruled. An ethnographer by training, Harrison's specific objective was to apply the same techniques of observation that he had used in studying the natives of Borneo to the study of the 'strange inhabitants' of England's northern industrial towns. Harrison lived incognito, as a participant-observer in Bolton, and subsequently built up a network of voluntary observers and correspondents who reported to a central registry on the popular customs they had observed, their friends' and neighbours' attitudes to such events as the abdication crisis, the bric-à-brac with which people adorned their living rooms, even their dreams. The studies which resulted offer a fascinating, albeit curious, body of evidence about the cultural life of significant sections of both the working and middle classes in the 1930s and 1940s (see Jeffery, 1978, for an excellent survey of Mass Observation).

While it is necessary to recognize such exceptions – and there are others – their significance should not be exaggerated, for they did not entirely circumvent the 'field of force' exerted by the 'culture and civilization' tradition. The very concept of mass observation, for example, implies an acceptance of the contention that the basic cultural divisions are those between an élite, however defined, and the masses. More importantly, such exceptions did not result in the development of a rival body of theory about the nature of popular culture and its place within the culture of the whole which could compete with those provided by the 'culture and civilization' and 'mass society' traditions. At this level, these reigned supreme.

However, perhaps the most telling index of the predominance of nineteenth-century traditions has been the extent to which, although pre-eminently conservative in hue, they have been able to pull in support from the left. Indeed, it is a singular paradox that, until recently, the Marxist analysis of popular culture – to the extent that it existed at all – proceeded within the terms of reference supplied by the 'culture and civilization' and 'mass society' traditions, borrowing their vocabulary and their constituent series of oppositions – between the folk and the masses, and so on – to develop a critique of the media as instruments of ruling-class ideological and cultural domination. The only difference between right and left in this respect consisted in their discrepant systems of political evaluation; they disapproved of the same things but for different reasons. 'Mass culture' was deplored on the left not so much because it sacrificed the values of culture as because it contributed to the depoliticization of the working classes, and because, far from only tenuously maintaining social authority, it did so only too well.

The issues involved here are most clearly exemplified in the work of the Frankfurt School. The most important figures here are Max Horkheimer, Theodor Adorno and Herbert Marcuse. Originally attached to the Frankfurt Institute for Social Research, founded in 1923, these scholars were forced into exile when Hitler became German Chancellor in 1933. Emigrating to America, the Institute was affiliated to the Sociology Department of the University of Columbia, where its researches into popular culture, already begun in Germany, were to continue to be developed in close association with the Office of Radio Research headed by Paul Lazarsfeld. It would be too arduous an undertaking to attempt, here, to deal adequately with the complexities of the Frankfurt School (see, however, Jay, 1973, and Slater, 1977, for useful surveys). Suffice it to say that, in a series of studies originating in the 1930s and, in the case of Marcuse, reaching right up to the present, the Frankfurt theorists radically re-vamped the mass society critique by integrating its constitutive elements within an analysis of monopoly capitalism, which was centrally concerned with the ability of what Adorno and Horkheimer called 'the culture industry' (see Adorno and Horkheimer, 1973) to mute or contain all sources of opposition. The standardized and formulaic nature of mass cultural production, its contamination and subversion of the critical values embodied in serious art and literature, the tendency towards an increasing intellectual and cultural mediocrity and homogeneity: all of these aspects of cultural pessimism – and often in their most acutely penetrating form – can be found in the writings of the Frankfurt theorists. But they are, so to speak, made to stand on their head in being addressed from the opposite direction. For what motivated the Frankfurt theorists' interest in these questions was not a crisis in social authority, but quite the reverse – the failure of the working classes in advanced capitalist countries even to 'think' of the possibility of revolution. Crudely put, they argued that the incorporation of the working classes into the structure of advanced capitalism, the limiting of their horizons to political and economic goals that could be realized within the capitalist system without challenging it, had been greatly facilitated by the development of the 'culture industry', given its ability to ideologically inoculate the masses against socialist ideas at the same time as and, indeed, by means of entertaining them.

You might find it helpful, at this point, to try to formulate some of the central weaknesses of the 'culture and civilization' tradition as they have been presented in Sections 2 and 4 of this unit.

5 The formation of the 'cultural studies' approach

5.1 The moment of transition

My main concern so far in this unit has been to convey some 'feel' of the 'culture and civilization' tradition by considering the way in which the political concerns expressed within it were related to a series of changes – social, political and cultural – associated with the development of industrial capitalism. There is not space here for a thorough-going criticism of this tradition. Its principal shortcomings, however, are:

1   An inadequate sense of historical periodization. The concept of a cultural fall with which the tradition operates has involved contrasting the state of culture as between a 'before' and an 'after'. The central difficulty has been that it has proved impossible to date these periods with any degree of accuracy or consistency. Put simply, one critic's 'after' has been another's 'before', as the boundary lines separating the pre- and post-fall stages of the culture have been shunted around in being located, variously, anywhere from Elizabethan England (Leavis) to the 1930s (Hoggart).

2   An uncritical acceptance of the standards of 'high culture'. These have, for the greater part, simply been assumed and have provided the critical norms in relation to which popular culture has been tried and found wanting, with the result that analysis has been unduly restricted by and to the somewhat narrow terms of reference of the socially dominant views of culture.

3   A lack of conceptual and methodological precision. Throughout the greater part of the tradition, such key terms as 'mass culture' or 'popular culture' have been used with a notable lack of regard for any degree of definitional precision while, so far as the analysis of forms of popular culture is concerned, it has been assumed that this is a relatively easy task which poses no special difficulties of a theoretical or methodological kind.

This is not to suggest that the 'culture and civilization' tradition can or should simply be dismissed. Whatever its failings, the questions it raised *were* ones concerning the relationships between culture and politics. Furthermore, although a predominantly conservative tradition in the sense that it contrasted the present unfavourably with an imaginary past, its criticisms of industrial capitalism *were* radical and far-reaching. The cultural diet of the people may have been deplored, but the responsibility for this was attributed clearly to the organization of culture along capitalist lines – the production of culture for profit – and rarely, if at all, to the people themselves. The achievement of Leavis, Francis Mulhern has argued, was that his work 'opened up an educational space within which the cultural institutions of bourgeois-democratic capitalism could be subjected to critical analysis' (Mulhern, 1979, p.329). Further, as Raymond Williams has subsequently corroborated in *Politics and Letters*, that space was considerably to the left of those available within either the Labour or the Communist parties during the height of the Cold War era. It is not surprising, therefore, that the origins of new approaches to the study of popular culture in this country should have emerged from within the womb of Leavisism.

It is in this sense that the late 1950s can be viewed as a 'moment of transition', a period in which new lines of approach to the study of popular culture continued to be informed – and impeded – by the inherited concerns of the 'culture and civilization' tradition. Nonetheless, the umbilical cord has since been cut. The principal characteristic of developments over the past two decades has been the emergence of approaches to the study of popular culture – mainly Marxist, or developed in a dialogue with Marxism – which have escaped or stood to one side of the gravitational pull which the 'culture and civilization' tradition had exerted on earlier Marxist overtures in this field. In order to appreciate the significance of these developments and place them in their proper context, however, they must be viewed as reacting against *both* the 'culture and civilization' tradition *and* earlier forms of Marxist cultural analysis. It is this double rejection that has marked the formation of what we earlier termed the 'cultural studies' approach (see p.6). The principal problem with regard to earlier Marxist formulations, except for those of the Frankfurt School, has been the potentially reductive implications of the base-superstructure conception according to which culture is assigned to the level of society's superstructure and, as such, held to be dependent on and determined by the economic relationships which comprise its 'base' (see Units 1/2 *Popular culture: defining our terms*, Section 3). This is a view which, if adhered to strictly, is both analytically and politically disabling: analytically disabling because it impedes an analysis of those properties that are peculiar to cultural forms — properties of genre, say — and which cannot simply be derived from a study of economic relationships, and politically disabling because it would seem to deny that culture plays any effective or autonomous role in social and political processes. The distinctive concern of the 'cultural studies' approach, accordingly, has been with the problem of the 'relative autonomy' of culture; that is, with devising ways in which it is possible to think about culture such that both its *separation from* (its autonomy) and its *connection with* (in the sense of both its dependency on and its consequences for) other social, economic and political processes might be recognized and taken account of. Two critical stages in the development of the cultural studies approach can be distinguished:

1   Firstly there appeared, in 1957 and 1961 respectively, Richard Hoggart's *The Uses of Literacy* and Raymond Williams's *The Long Revolution* — works which, as Stuart Hall has put it, 'form the break, the turning point from which a new area of study opens' (Hall, 1978, p.16). The significance of these studies, the conservatism of Hoggart's work notwithstanding, was the claim they advanced to the effect that the 'lived cultures' of ordinary people were worthy of study in their own right. If Hoggart made this claim in a practical way by actually evoking the 'lived culture' of his working-class childhood, Williams provided the theoretical justification for this expansion of the scope and concerns of the study of culture. He did so by extending the available definitions of the term 'culture' beyond its traditional restricted usage to include 'the "social" definition of culture, in which culture is a description of a particular way of life, which expresses certain meanings and values not only in art and learning but also in institutions and ordinary behaviour' (Williams, 1961 p.43 in Reader 2). On this basis, Williams went on to define 'the theory of culture as the study of relationships between elements in a whole way of life' and the 'analysis of culture' as 'the attempt to discover the nature of the organization which is the complex of these relationships' (ibid. p.47).

The impact of these theoretical reorientations has been registered chiefly in history and sociology. In both cases, the main concern has been to interrogate the distinctive 'lived cultures' of different sections of the working class, past and present, in order to identify the 'structure of feelings' said to be contained or expressed within them. The work of historians has concentrated principally on the adult culture of different sections of the nineteenth-century working class, the model here being E.P. Thompson's *The Making of the English Working Class*. Sociologists, by contrast, have chiefly been concerned with what has been dubbed the 'spectacular subcultures' of post-war working-class male youth — teddy boys, mods, rockers, skinheads. These two areas of work comprise the distinctively 'home-grown' contribution to the development of cultural studies in Britain over the past quarter of a century, a contribution that has been characterized by a distinctive theoretical logic governing the way in which the relationship between cultural form and class situation is viewed. Briefly, culture is regarded as 'that level at which social groups develop distinct patterns of life, and give *expressive form* to their social and material life experience' (Hall and Jefferson, 1976, p.10). The distinctive forms and practices which constitute the cultural 'way of life' of a class are, that is to say, construed as in some way expressing or giving formal coherence to the socially moulded experience and perspectives of the members of that class.

2   As the sixties progressed and, more particularly, since the seventies, the development of cultural theory in Britain has been profoundly influenced by the translation

of a wide-ranging body of European cultural theory, conventionally known as 'structuralism', which proposes terms for the analysis of cultural forms which differ significantly from those developed within the home-grown or 'culturalist' tradition.

The key figures in this respect have been Roland Barthes, whose impact has been registered chiefly in the areas of film and literary criticism; Claude Lévi-Strauss, whose work on the myths and customs of 'primitive' peoples has profoundly modified anthropological and sociological approaches to the study of culture; Jacques Lacan, whose revision of the Freudian theory of psychoanalysis has led to important new lines of approach to the study of film and literature; and Louis Althusser, especially with regard to his reformulation of the concept of ideology and of its place within Marxist theory. While there are important differences between these theorists, they are conventionally grouped together under the heading of 'structuralism' because of their characteristic emphasis on the underlying properties, or *structures*, which generate the surface appearances of cultural forms.

Of course, the notion that cultural forms exhibit patterned regularities which can be grasped as a 'structure' is not limited to structuralism; indeed, as we shall see shortly, the concept of 'structure of feelings' is a key concept within the culturalist tradition. What distinguishes structuralism is the claim that such patterned regularities exhibit properties similar to those discernible within the organization of language and that they may, accordingly, be unearthed by the use of similar methodological tools. As a form of analysis, therefore, structuralism tends to focus on the compositional and structural properties which govern the internal formal organization of particular cultural forms and, in its initial phases, made little attempt to connect or relate these to the relevant social and historical contexts. In more recent years, this one-sided emphasis has been corrected as, within Marxist circles, the principles of structuralism have been both modified and extended so as to enable such social and historical considerations to be taken into account.

Structuralism has largely derived its inspiration from the work of Ferdinand de Saussure, the founder of modern linguistics (the study of language). The significance of Saussure's work (discussed more fully in Unit 14), from the point of view of our concerns here, consists in his suggestion that the organization of language should not be viewed as the product or expression of the thoughts or feelings of language users. To the contrary, Saussure argued, meaning is produced within language solely by virtue of the rules which govern the permissible combination of linguistic terms, and it is this, the pre-given structure of language, that produces and organizes the thought and feelings — the speech — of language users. By extension, those who have worked within the tradition opened up by Saussure have argued that *all* cultural forms — film, novels, fashion systems, the customs and rituals comprising 'lived cultures' — exhibit a similar logic. It can easily be seen how, if this is so, the validity of treating any cultural form as expressing, organizing or giving coherence to the thoughts or experience of an individual, or the members of a social group or class, is contested. For it is to imply that the logic of analysis should be entirely the reverse of this. Such cultural forms should, according to structuralist canons, be analysed to reveal the way in which their organization works so as actively to *produce* the thoughts and experiences, the consciousness, of those who are subjected to their action.

In summary, then, the 'cultural studies' approach, as it has been developed since the 1960s, consists of two contending *paradigms* or systems of explanation — the 'culturalist' and the 'structuralist'. These can be grouped together as part of a joint 'cultural studies' approach in the respect that they are both, broadly speaking, Marxist and, as contrasted with earlier Marxist approaches to the study of culture, have been concerned to devise ways in which the interaction between cultural forms and economic, social and political processes might be analysed while, at the same time, acknowledging the specificity and autonomy of the former. Where they differ is with regard to their estimations of the ways in which this might be done.

5.2 Culturalism and structuralism

In this section, I want you to form some impressions of your own of the differences between 'culturalism and 'structuralism' by reading two pieces which exemplify these approaches. The first, 'The analysis of culture' is taken from Raymond Williams's *The Long Revolution*. The second, 'The study of ideologies and philosophy of language', is taken from V.N. Volosinov's *Marxism and the Philosophy of Language*. Both are contained in Reader 2. The contexts in which these two pieces were written, it should be noted, are quite different. *The Long Revolution*, first published in 1961, was the work in which Williams tried to fill the space that his earlier criticisms of both the 'culture and civilization' tradition and of reductive Marxist formulations had created. Volosinov's work, by contrast, was first published in 1929. But it, too, was intended as a polemic against reductionism in its specific manifestation, in early Soviet linguistics, in the view that language was a mere reflex of society's economic base. Its interest, from our point of view, is that it opposed to this view arguments and perspectives derived from the tradition of structural linguistics associated with Ferdinand de Saussure, albeit that these were, in their turn, subjected to criticisms and modification in being assimilated within a Marxist framework. Although both Williams and Volosinov are thus concerned to oppose reductionist views of, respectively, culture and language, they do so in notably different ways – although not totally different ways. Interestingly, since writing *The Long Revolution*, Williams has revised some of his earlier positions in the light of his subsequent familiarity with Volosinov's work. However, it is the differences with which we are concerned at the moment.

You should now read 'The analysis of culture', pp.43–52 in Reader 2. In doing so, try to answer the following questions:

1 What is the nature of Williams's objection to determinist accounts of culture?
2 What does Williams mean by the concept of 'structure of feeling'?
3 How is the relation between a 'structure of feeling' and the 'documentary forms' of a culture viewed?
4 What, in Williams's view, is the end purpose of analysing the 'documentary forms' of a culture?

Comments

1 Williams argues that it is mistaken to accord priority to any area of life (such as society or the economy) if, as a result, another area of life (such as culture) is viewed as its mere by-product or reflection. Since culture forms a part of society, there is no point abstracting the two and conceding priority to the latter since, by definition, social relationships cannot be understood independently of cultural relationships. Because the two reciprocally affect and underpin or determine one another, Williams argues, it is the dynamic and complex organization of the relationships between them that should be studied.

2 The concept of 'structure of feeling' is a difficult one to pin down partly because Williams himself uses it hesitatingly and with subtle variations of meaning. The general idea, however, is that of a shared set of ways of thinking and feeling which, displaying a patterned regularity, form and are formed by the 'whole way of life' which comprises the 'lived culture' of a particular epoch, social class or group. A 'structure of feeling' is culture as it is lived by groups of individuals who share the same experiences and social and historical situation. Although hesitatingly, Williams's discussion of this concept clearly introduces the notion of a distinction between dominant and subordinate cultures, important concepts in his later writings.

The 'structure of feeling' of an epoch, he argues, is in one sense 'the culture of a period: it is the particular living result of all the elements in the general organization' (p.48). The sort of patterned regularities which such a structure of feeling displays are, however, viewed as being governed by the 'social character' – the valued system of behaviour and attitudes – of the dominant social group. Although this 'dominant social character' – consisting of those ways of thought and feeling that emanate from the socially dominant class and which are consonant with its interests, its view of itself and of its relationships to other classes – is to a degree shared by all classes, its distribution is nevertheless uneven. There exist other patterns of thought and ways of feeling which are opposed to or only partly in line with the 'dominant social character', and it is within the interaction between these that the peculiar shape or organization of the 'structure of feeling' of a period is to be deciphered. It is in this way that Williams registers the effects of class divisions in the sphere of culture, viewing the latter as a set of relations between the cultures of different groups that is unequally structured by the dominance of the culture of the ruling group or class.

3   The documentary forms of a culture – that is, culture that takes the form of durable artefacts, 'from poems to buildings and dress fashions' (p.49) – are viewed as the 'carriers' of structures of feeling. They are the sedimented forms of culture as it is lived, the material forms in which structures of feeling are expressed and in which they survive 'when the living witnesses are silent' (p.49).

4   Regarded as the sedimented forms of a lived culture, documentary forms are to be analysed with a view to rediscovering, as closely as possible, the structure of feelings – be it of a class, or social group or of a whole period – informing the lived culture which served as their initial support. In practice, Williams admits, this is difficult: 'The most difficult thing to get hold of, in studying any past period, is this felt sense of the quality of life at a particular place and time: a sense of the ways in which the particular activities combined into a way of thinking and living' (p.48). In particular, the documentary forms of a culture are always absorbed into a 'selective tradition' and as such, are necessarily 'different from the culture as lived' (p.50). Given that any attempted rediscovery of a lived culture necessarily constitutes a selective interpretation of that culture, Williams suggests such interpretations should be consciously related to the contemporary values and interests on which they rest. Cultural analysis is an interpretation and attempted reconstruction of dormant or partially dormant lived cultures undertaken for and from within the interests and values of the present.

It is possible to extrapolate from the above some of the more distinctive and generally shared features of 'culturalism':

1   Culturalism, Stuart Hall has argued, 'is an attempt, through analysis, to recreate the whole set of tensions which are being "lived" (experienced) in any historical moment' (Hall, 1978, p.19). It is an attempt to get beneath the skin of a particular culture, to feel and think again what was once spontaneously thought and felt from within it. Culturalism is thus concerned with the interpretation or appropriation of meaning. It seeks to revivify dead cultural forms by breathing new interpretative life into them.

2   At the level of explanation, culturalism suggests that cultural forms should be viewed as the product, in whatever medium (print, song, film), of the structure of feelings which the members of a social group, class or period have in common as a result of shared life experiences – the basis for which is supplied by their shared social or historical situation. We can see here how the Marxist stress on the principle of determination is maintained. Culture is not free-floating: it is the expression of men's and women's consciousness which is, in turn, influenced and conditioned by the shared circumstances of their social being. But only influenced and conditioned; Williams avoids the reductive implications of the conventional base-superstructure formulation by the stress he places on *human agency*, on men and women *making* their culture by responding to the situations in which they find themselves, using the tools and materials available to them in a process of meaning-making which is always *active*. It is in this sense that, in his later writings, Williams has argued that the concept of determination should be understood as a 'setting of limits'; it supplies the conditions within which human practice must be located but does not dictate its results.

You should now read Volosinov's 'The study of ideologies and the philosophy of language', pp.145–52 in Reader 2, paying particular attention to the following questions:

1   How does Volosinov view the relationship between ideology and other areas of social reality?

2   What does Volosinov mean when he says: 'Individual consciousness is not the architect of the ideological superstructure, but only a tenant lodging in the edifice of ideological signs'?

3   How does this contrast with Williams's view of the relationship between cultural form and consciousness?

4   How does Volosinov view the relationship between the ideological superstructure and the economic basis of society?

Comments

1   One of the more innovative aspects of Volosinov's work is his insistence that ideology – the world of signs – is just as real, just as physical and material, as any other aspect of reality. The study of ideology, thus defined, does not consist in the study of subjective, hidden-from-view states or processes of consciousness, but is rather the study of observable material processes – the manipulation of signs in specific ways in specific contexts.

2   The sign is distinguished from ordinary physical objects, however, by its functioning, by the fact that it is 'not only itself a part of reality' but 'reflects and refracts another reality outside itself' (p.145); by the fact, that is, that it possesses meaning, that it signifies, 'represents, depicts, or stands for something lying outside itself' (p.145). The relationship between ideology, or the world of signs, and other areas of social life, is thus one of representation or *signification*. The autonomy or relative independence of ideology is secured in the claim that 'each field of ideological creativity has its own kind of orientation towards reality and each refracts reality in its own way, (p.147).

3   Writing against idealist accounts of the relationship between language and consciousness, Volosinov argues for a reversal of the more usual way of viewing the relationship between the world of signs (or ideology or culture) and consciousness. Within idealist philosophies of culture, according to Volosinov, signs are viewed as the means through which the inner thoughts and feelings of individuals are expressed. The world of signs is the external, objective manifestation of the inner world of consciousness. This concept of an inner world of consciousness is, Volosinov suggests, a fiction: 'consciousness can arise and become a viable fact only in the material embodiment of signs' (p.147). Particular ideologies and cultural forms, Volosinov argues, cannot be viewed as the organized expression of the already existing consciousness of men and women. This is because, according to Volosinov, consciousness can have no existence prior to the ways in which it is produced and organized by the operation *on* men and women of particular ideologies or cultural forms. There is a clear tension between this account of the relationships between consciousness and culture and Williams's view that what he calls the documentary forms of a culture are to be regarded as expressions of the ways of thought and feeling which comprise any given 'structure of feeling'.

4   While allowing that each field of ideological creativity displays its own kind of orientation towards reality, Volosinov retains the Marxist stress on the economic-conditioning of ideology by suggesting that the specific form of any ideology is determined by the conditions of social intercourse, of inter-individual communication, in which it is generated. These, in turn, 'are directly determined by the total aggregate of social and economic laws' (p.149).

Again, it is possible to extrapolate some of the more generally shared aspects of 'structuralism' from the above and to indicate the respects in which they differ from 'culturalism':

1   Structuralism is characterized by its rejection of the concerns of interpretative analysis. Whereas culturalism seeks to harvest particular meanings from specific cultural and ideological forms, structuralism is centrally concerned with the formal means and mechanisms whereby such forms work so as to *produce* meanings for those influenced by them.

2   Culturalism is founded on the assumption that any given cultural practice can be explained by referring it back to the consciousness or experience of some 'subject' which is held to constitute its point of origin. This 'subject' may be conceived of as an individual (the author of a novel, for example) or as a 'collective subject' (as when particular sets of values are attributed to a social group). Alternatively, an individual may be construed as *representing* a collective subject, as when it is claimed – as it frequently is – that Tolstoy's works gave literary expression to the collective world view of the Russian peasantry. Whichever the case, however, the logic of analysis is the same. A novel, a film, a song, a style of fashion: all cultural forms, within the logic of culturalism, are held to give form or expression to the sentiments, values, world view or structure of feeling of a particular individual or of a group of individuals construed as a collective thinking and feeling subject because of their shared experiences and circumstances. Structuralism, by contrast, denies that there is any such 'subject' to which there might be attributed forms of consciousness, world views or

structures of feeling prior to or independent of the ways in which these are organized within particular ideological forms.

3   The two approaches construe the relative autonomy of culture differently. Within culturalism this is secured by the active role assigned to human agency as the key mediating link between determined conditions and resulting cultural form. Within structuralism, the relative autonomy of culture is secured via the insistence that each different sphere of culture – art, religion, philosophy – is governed by properties peculiar to itself with the result that each signifies or represents reality differently.

4   This is linked to a difference in orientation between the two approaches. Whereas culturalism is more concerned with explaining culture with reference to its roots in some originating social milieux (such as the shared perspectives of a class), the stress within structuralism falls on calculating the political consequences or effects that might be attributed to particular ideologies or cultural forms in view of the impact they might be expected to have on the consciousness of those who are exposed to or influenced by them.

In order to grasp more concretely the somewhat abstract considerations outlined above, you might find it helpful to look back through the materials comprising the Christmas case study with a view to determining which of the approaches used in it might·be categorized as 'structuralist' and which as 'culturalist'. 'Taking the biscuit', the article by Douglas and Nicod, is clearly structuralist in orientation, for example. It is concerned with the internal rules governing a particular dietary system and not at all with the meanings of that system for those whose eating practices are governed by it. The extracts from James Barnett's *The American Christmas*, by contrast, are not at all concerned with the formal description of rules of this kind. Rather, Barnett tries to *read through* the various customs and rituals he describes in order to distil the meanings these might have for those who take part in them.

It might be said, in conclusion, that culturalism and structuralism are principally distinguishable in terms of their contrasting approaches to the question of meaning. For culturalism, the *interpretation* of meaning is a process to be *engaged in*; for structuralism, the *production of* meaning is a process to be *analysed*. It is worth noting, in connection with this, that Volosinov's work has played an important role in challenging the often a-historical and a-social nature of some of the purer forms of structuralism. Volosinov's comments on what he called 'the necessary social multi-accentuality of the sign', according to which signs are viewed as being liable to different interpretations by different social groups, have been particularly influential in this respect. For Volosinov, the production of meaning is regarded as always being a *contested* process, a matter for struggle between different classes, races, age groups and, of course, genders.

   This perspective on culture as a sphere of struggle and contest introduces the last concept that I should like to discuss in this unit – that of *hegemony*. This concept is associated with the work of the Italian Marxist, Antonio Gramsci, who developed his thoughts on this subject in *Prison Notebooks*, written between 1929 and 1935 during his incarceration in a fascist prison at Turi in Southern Italy. Although in developing the concept Gramsci was principally concerned with questions of political strategy, it has since exerted an enormous influence on Marxist theories of culture. However, it is, with regard to the relations between 'culturalism' and 'structuralism', something of a joker in the pack, cutting across the opposition between them in its concern, not with how to analyse particular forms of culture, but with how to understand the ways in which the cultures and ideologies of different classes are related to one another within any given social and historical situation.

5.3   Hegemony and popular culture

We have already noted the problem of reductionism associated with the Marxist concept of ideology. Consideration must now be given to the related problem of *domination*. Marx and Engels wrote that 'the ruling *material* force in society, is at the same time its ruling *intellectual* force' (see Units 1/2 *Popular culture: defining our*

terms, Section 3). This suggests that the ideology of the dominant class is simply *imposed* on the members of subordinate classes who, in their turn, *passively acquiesce* in this. It was against such a view that Gramsci developed his concept of hegemony, arguing for a more dynamic and flexible conception of the ways in which the relationships between dominant and subordinate classes are ordered.

Read the introduction to the 'Passages from Gramsci' collected in Reader 2 (pp.191–3), and the passages grouped under the heading 'Hegemony' (pp.197–9) and try to answer the following questions.

1   What distinction does Gramsci draw between the notions of *leadership* and *domination*?
2   Under what conditions does a 'fundamental social group' exert hegemony?
3   How is a 'crisis of social authority' defined? What might be the consequences of such a crisis?

Comments

1   A condition of hegemony exists when a 'fundamental social class' (that is, a class which plays a 'decisive function' in 'the decisive nucleus of economic activity' – the bourgeoisie or the working class within capitalist society) exerts *moral* and *intellectual leadership* over both allied and subordinate social classes. This is contrasted with a situation in which a class merely *rules*; that is, *coercively imposes* its will on other classes.

2   Such a condition is secured when a dominant class is able, by moral and intellectual means, to co-ordinate the interests of subordinate and allied classes with its own. Under such circumstances, the subordinate classes in society, to a degree, actively subscribe to the values and objectives of the dominant class rather than have these simply imposed on them. This consent, however, is not guaranteed. Nor can its existence simply be assumed. It has, on the contrary, incessantly to be produced. In this sense, hegemony refers not to an achieved state, but to a process: to those ideological processes whereby such consent is continually reproduced and secured – or lost.

3   Hegemony, then, refers to a condition in which the dominant class does not merely *rule*, but *leads* society; moments in which it enjoys a degree of moral, social and intellectual authority such that its right to govern is not seriously challenged. Such periods are characterized by a high degree of consensus and, consequently, social stability and equilibrium – not in the sense that there are no conflicts, but in the sense that such conflicts as do occur are bounded in scope by the terms of reference supplied by the dominant ideology and, consequently, fail to touch the essentials of class power. More than that, the concept refers to situations in which the ruling bloc has been able to mobilize the people *actively* to support its objectives.

4   It is, by contrast, a breach in the consensual terms of reference supplied by the dominant ideology that signals a crisis of hegemony:

> A crisis of hegemony marks a moment of profound rupture in the political and economic life of a society, an accumulation of contradictions. If in moments of 'hegemony' everything works spontaneously so as to sustain and enforce a particular form of class domination while rendering the basis of that social authority invisible through the mechanisms of the production of consent, the moments when the equilibrium of consent is disturbed . . . are moments *when the whole basis of political leadership and cultural authority becomes exposed and contested.*
>
> (Hall *et al*, 1978, p.217)

The causes of such crises of hegemony may be numerous and diverse. For Gramsci, such crises may occur 'either because the ruling class has failed in some major political undertaking for which it has requested, or forcibly extracted, the consent of the broad masses (war, for example), or because huge masses (especially of peasants and *petit bourgeois* intellectuals) have passed suddenly from a state of political passivity to a certain activity, and put forward demands which taken together, albeit not organically formulated, add up to a revolution' (Gramsci, 1971, p.210). More generally, economic crises have been held to be the acid test of hegemony. Whether or not such crises result in an open political contestation of the ruling class's social authority, however, depends on the extent to which the dominant class is capable, in such situations, of continuing to limit popular struggles and aspirations within acceptable bounds – such as, say, the routinized struggle over the size of the wage packet – or whether, to the contrary, these move beyond such limits to challenge the distribution of economic and political power within society as a whole. Whatever the causes, however, such crises of hegemony, Gramsci argued, result in the more active and open use of more directly coercive forms of domination. The dominant class may, in such circumstances, *rule* but it no longer *leads*.

It can easily be seen how this concept of *hegemony* differs from the notion of simple domination. The process of *winning consent* which it refers to 'is more complex than the dissemination downwards in society of a single, dominant "class world view" ' (Gray, 1976, p.5). In contrast to domination as 'a static and omnipotent system', it refers to 'an on-going and problematic historical process'; not a simple imposition of dominant ideologies on subordinate classes but an active *reaching into* and *structuring* of the culture and experience of subordinate classes. As Robert Gray summarizes:

> Class hegemony is a dynamic and shifting relationship of social subordination, which operates in two directions. Certain aspects of the behaviour and consciousness of the subordinate classes may reproduce a version of the values of the ruling class. But in the process value systems are modified, through their necessary adaptation to diverse conditions of existence; the subordinate classes thus follow a 'negotiated version' of ruling-class values. On the other hand, structures of ideological hegemony transform and incorporate dissident values, so as effectively to prevent the working through of their full implications.
>
> (Gray, 1976, p.6)

Well, that's no more than a brief look at a complicated concept. But it is one that will play an important part in many of the debates you will be concerned with in later parts of the course. It is easy to see how, in the first instance, the sphere of popular culture occupies an important place within the processes whereby hegemony is secured – or lost. If the ruling class is to *lead* and not merely rule, if it is to enjoy social, moral and intellectual authority over the whole of society, then its views must reach into and be influential in 'framing' the ways in which, at the level of culture, the members of subordinate classes 'live', experience or respond to their social situation. It is in this respect that the concept of hegemony provides a useful way in which we might think about the ways in which developments within the sphere of popular culture might be connected with more general political and ideological processes. It also provides a possible way out from the definitional dilemmas outlined in Units 1/2. At the end of Units 1/2 it was suggested that we needed a view of popular culture that fell somewhere in-between the view of popular culture as an 'imposed from above' mass culture, and popular culture as an 'emerging from below', spontaneously oppositional culture. It was also suggested that, to do this, popular culture needed to be viewed as an *area of exchange* between the culture and ideology of the dominant classes in society and the culture and ideology of subordinate classes. The concept of hegemony affords one way of doing this, suggesting that within the sphere of popular culture there takes place a series of *transactions* between the culture and ideology of society's ruling groups and those of the subordinate classes as, through state or commercially provided forms of popular culture, the former reaches into the latter, redefining and re-shaping it only to be partially accepted, opposed, resisted, turned against itself, and so on. It suggests that the field of popular culture is one *structured* by the attempt to win consent to or compliance with dominant ideology, and by forms of opposition to such attempts. As such it consists not simply of an imposed mass culture that is consonant with the interests of the dominant class, nor simply of a spontaneously oppositional working-class culture; it is rather an *area of negotiation* between the two within which – in different forms of popular culture – dominant, subordinate and oppositional elements are 'mixed' in different combinations.

This interpretation could be placed on the concept of popular culture as a general category applicable to the non-official cultures of all historical periods. The implication of the foregoing has been to suggest that the peculiarity of popular culture in

31

industrial societies is determined by the critical role played by the state and by commercial mechanisms – as contrasted with, for example, the key role of religious institutions or the structures of patronage in earlier periods – in organizing the cultural and ideological relationships and transactions between dominant and subordinate classes.

However, the concept also plays an important part in the historical concerns of the course in another way. One of our central objectives in this course is to offer you a synoptic perspective on the development of popular culture in Britain from the early nineteenth century to the present, and to relate such developments to the broader social, political and historical processes of which they formed a part. The concept of hegemony will play an important part in these debates. With regard to recent history, it has been argued by Stuart Hall and his colleagues that Britain has been undergoing a crisis of social authority – which we can now redefine as a crisis of hegemony – during the period since the 1960s. In Block 5, we shall consider the implications of this thesis for the ways in which the salient developments in the sphere of popular culture over the same period might be viewed. More immediately, we turn our attention to the nineteenth century.

By now you may be aware that the perspective on the historical development of popular culture offered in Section 3 of this unit is implicitly informed by the concept of hegemony. Try to work out how by jotting down how the transition from the late eighteenth to the late nineteenth century, outlined in Section 3 of this unit, might be described in terms of the concept of hegemony.

In recent years, the concept of hegemony has played an important part in controversies between historians concerning the degree to and the mechanisms by which the social authority – the hegemony – of the ruling classes was maintained during the nineteenth century. One view – the one to which I have broadly subscribed in Section 3 – suggests that, whereas in the eighteenth century the landed classes were able to *lead* as opposed to merely *rule* subordinate social classes, the development of industrial capitalism in the first half of the nineteenth century witnessed a crisis of social authority – not in the sense that the ruling classes were unable to rule (their power to govern was never seriously placed in question), but in the sense that, as seen in the rise of Chartism, the exercise of such power rested on a diminished degree of popular consent. It was contested. This development, I have suggested, was paralleled – partly as cause, partly as consequence – by the shift from a plebeian popular culture that was closely controlled and influenced by the landed classes, to a working-class popular culture that was, to a considerable degree, removed from and opposed to the influence of the culture and ideology of the new industrial bourgeoisie. In the later half of the nineteenth century, the thesis goes on, the ruling classes were again able to lead as opposed to merely rule as a consequence of the development of new ideologies – specifically those of liberalism and imperialism – which were able, through a variety of routes, to influence and modify working-class culture. The development of new, commercial forms of popular culture, I have suggested, played an important part in this process.

In short, it has been suggested that developments within the sphere of popular culture played an important part in the process whereby hegemony was first lost and, subsequently, reconstructed in the nineteenth century. As Hugh Cunningham describes the situation at the end of this process:

> The outcome of a century of battles over the problem of leisure was that for the dominant culture leisure was safely residual, unconnected with and possibly a counterweight to new and socialist challenges to hegemony.
> (Cunningham, 1980, p.199)

It is to a further consideration of this thesis, and of alternative views, that we now turn in Block 2.

32

Checklist of study objectives

Because all of the issues discussed in this unit will be dealt with at greater length and with more detailed examples later in the course, all that you need to have acquired, at this stage, is a rough and ready sense of the major themes of the unit. As a way of pulling together your understanding of these, you might find it helpful to go back over the relevant parts of the unit and see how far you are able to:

1   outline the main themes of the 'culture and civilization' approach to the study of popular culture, to summarize its principal weaknesses and indicate the respects in which the development of this tradition was related to changes in the sphere of popular culture itself;

2   offer rough definitions for the terms 'culturalism' and 'structuralism' and to outline the key ways in which these approaches differ from one another;

3   outline the differences between the concepts of *hegemony* and *domination*;

4   summarize the ways in which the concept of hegemony suggests that the relationships between popular culture and broader social and political processes might be viewed.

Chapter 1 of Dick Hebdige's *Subcultures: The Meaning of Style* (set book) usefully complements many of the points discussed in this unit. You might find it helpful to read this now, or to do so when you come to revise this part of the course.

Further reading

This unit has introduced many different issues which you might like to follow up. If the broad contours of the historical development of popular culture are of interest to you, then the works by Burke, Malcolmson and Cunningham cited in the references are good starting points. Walvin, J. (1978) *Leisure and Society, 1830–1950* (Longman) is also worth a look. Clear and fuller statements of the relations between culturalism and structuralism can be found in Stuart Hall's 'Cultural studies: two paradigms' in Reader 2, and this is set reading for Unit 18. The bearing of the concept of hegemony on historical debates concerning the structure of authority in the nineteenth century is succinctly outlined in Gray's 'Bourgeois hegemony in Victorian Britain' in Reader 2, a set reading for Block 2. If you are interested in what I have called the 'culture and civilization' approach, A. Swingewood's *The Myth of Mass Culture* (1977, Macmillan) provides an accessible general survey while Francis Mulhern's *The Moment of Scrutiny* (1979, New Left Books) offers a compelling analysis of the specifically English manifestation of this approach as exemplified by Leavis and his associates.

References

ADORNO, T.W. and HORKHEIMER, M. (1973) 'The culture industry: enlightenment as mass deception' in Curran, J., Gurevitch, M. and Woollacott, J. (eds) (1977) *Mass Communication and Society*, Edward Arnold.

ARNOLD, M. (1971) *Culture and Anarchy*, Bobbs-Merrill (first published in 1869).

BENNETT, T., MARTIN, G., MERCER, C. and WOOLLACOTT, J.(eds) (1981) *Culture, Ideology and Social Process*, Batsford (Reader 2).

BURKE, P. (1978) *Popular Culture in Early Modern Europe*, Temple Smith.

CUNNINGHAM, H. (1980) *Leisure in the Industrial Revolution*, Croom Helm.

CURRAN, J. (1977) 'Capitalism and control of the press 1800–1975' in Curran, J., Gurevitch, M. and Woollacott, J. (eds) (1977) *Mass Communication and Society*, Edward Arnold.

FOSTER, J. (1974) *Class Struggle and the Industrial Revolution*, Methuen.

GRAMSCI, A. (1971) *Selections from the Prison Notebooks*, translated and edited by Hoare, Q. and Nowell-Smith, G., Lawrence and Wishart.

GRAY, R. (1976) *The Labour Aristocracy in Victorian Edinburgh*, Clarendon Press.

HALL, S. and JEFFERSON, T. (eds) (1976) *Resistance through Rituals: Youth Subcultures in Post-war Britain*, Hutchinson.

HALL, S. (1978) 'Some paradigms in cultural studies', *Annali*, Vol.3.

HALL, S., CRITCHER, C., JEFFERSON, T., CLARKE, J. and ROBERTS, B. (1978) *Policing the Crisis: Mugging, the State and Law and Order*, Macmillan.

HEBDIGE, D. (1979) *Subculture: The Meaning of Style*, Methuen (set book).

HOBSBAWM, E.J. (1969) *Industry and Empire*, Penguin.

JAMES, L. (1974) *Fiction for the Working Man*, Penguin.

JAY, M. (1973) *The Dialectical Imagination: A History of the Frankfurt School and the Institute of Social Research*, Heinemann.

JEFFERY, T. (1978) 'Mass Observation – a short history' in *CCCS Working Papers in Cultural Studies*, No.55, Birmingham University.

JOHNSON, R. (1979) ' "Really useful knowledge": radical education and working-class culture' in Clarke, J. and Johnson, R. (eds) *Working-class Culture: Studies in History and Theory*, Hutchinson.

LEAVIS, Q.D. (1932) *Fiction and the Reading Public*, Chatto and Windus.

LEAVIS, F.R. and THOMPSON, D. (1933) *Culture and Environment*, Chatto and Windus.

LLOYD, A.L. (1975) *Folk Song in England*, Paladin.

MALCOLMSON, R. (1973) *Popular Recreations in English Society 1700–1850*, Cambridge University Press.

MULHERN, F. (1979) *The Moment of 'Scrutiny'*, New Left Books.

PAINE, T. (1791) *Rights of Man*, reissued by Penguin, 1976.

SLATER, P. (1977) *The Origin and Significance of the Frankfurt School*, Routledge and Kegan Paul.

STEDMAN-JONES, G. (1976) *Outcast London: A Study in the Relationship between Classes in Victorian Society*, Penguin.

THOMPSON, E.P. (1968) *The Making of the English Working Class*, Penguin.

THOMPSON, E.P. (1971) 'The moral economy of the English crowd in the eighteenth century', *Past and Present*, No. 50.

THOMPSON, E.P. (1974) 'Patrician society, plebeian culture', *Journal of Social History*, Vol.VII, No.4.

THOMPSON, E.P. (1978) 'Eighteenth-century English society: class struggle without class?', *Journal of Social History*, Vol.III, No.2.

WAITES, B., BENNETT, T. and MARTIN, G. (eds) (1981) *Popular Culture: Past and Present*, Croom Helm (Reader 1).

WILLIAMS, R. (1958) *Culture and Society 1780-1950*, Chatto and Windus.

WILLIAMS, R. (1979) *Politics and Letters*, New Left Books.